W9-BAG-311

Graphs with Giraffes

GS
MATH

By Ethan Weingarten

Please visit our website, www.garethstevens.com. For a free color catalog of all our high-quality books, call toll free 1-800-542-2595 or fax 1-877-542-2596.

Library of Congress Cataloging-in-Publication Data

Weingarten, Ethan.
Graphs with giraffes / by Ethan Weingarten.
    p. cm. — (Animal math)
Includes index.
ISBN 978-1-4339-9314-5 (pbk.)
ISBN 978-1-4339-9315-2 (6-pack)
ISBN 978-1-4339-9313-8 (library binding)
1. Graphic methods—Juvenile literature. 2. Giraffe—Juvenile literature. I. Weingarten, Ethan II. Title.
QA90.W45 2014
518.23—dc23

First Edition

Published in 2014 by
Gareth Stevens Publishing
111 East 14th Street, Suite 349
New York, NY 10003

Copyright © 2014 Gareth Stevens Publishing

Designer: Nicholas Domiano
Editor: Therese M. Shea

Photo credits: Cover, p. 1 Rich Carey/Shutterstock.com; pp. 3–24 (background texture) Natutik/Shutterstock.com; p. 5 Zoonar/Thinkstock.com; pp. 6, 8, 10, 16 iStockphoto/Thinkstock.com; pp. 7, 13, 17, 18 iStockphoto/Thinkstock.com; p. 9 stockpix4u/Shutterstock.com; p. 11 Hemera/Thinkstock.com; p. 14 falk/Shutterstock.com; pp. 15, 21 Comstock/Thinkstock.com; p. 19 © iStockphoto.com/mehmettorlak; p. 21 Katrina Brown/Shutterstock.com;

Printed in the United States of America

CPSIA compliance information: Batch #CS13GS: For further information contact Gareth Stevens, New York, New York at 1-800-542-2595.

Contents

Boldface words appear in the glossary.

Giraffes and Graphs

Graphs help us count and **compare**. Let's learn about giraffes with graphs. Check your answers on page 22.

Look at the graph. How many giraffes are at Big City Zoo? How many are at Little City Zoo?

Giraffes at the Zoo

 =1

Big City Zoo   Little City Zoo

Hello Up There!

Giraffes are the tallest animals on land! This bar graph compares a man and a giraffe. The bottom of the graph tells who. The left side of the graph tells how tall.

How tall is the giraffe?

Who's Taller?

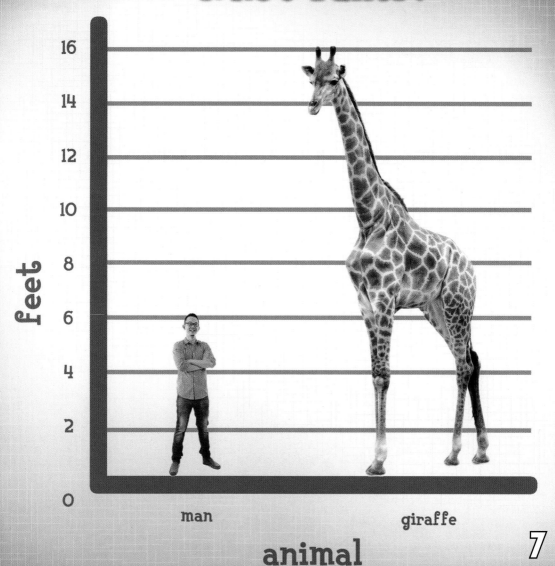

feet

16
14
12
10
8
6
4
2
0

man   giraffe

animal

7

Even baby giraffes are tall!

Read the bar graph. Who is taller, the child or the baby giraffe? Is the baby giraffe smaller than the man or the same size?

Who's Taller?

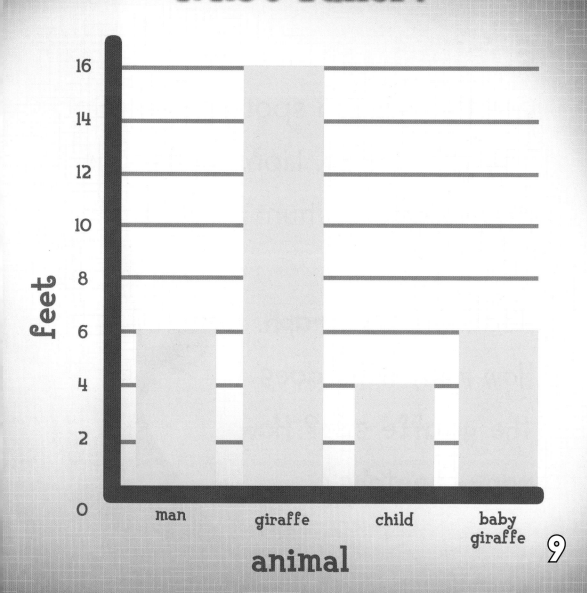

Spotted

Giraffes have a spotted coat. Spots help them hide. Lions, **cheetahs**, and crocodiles hunt giraffes.

Read the bar graph. How many lions does the giraffe see? How many cheetahs?

What Does the Giraffe See?

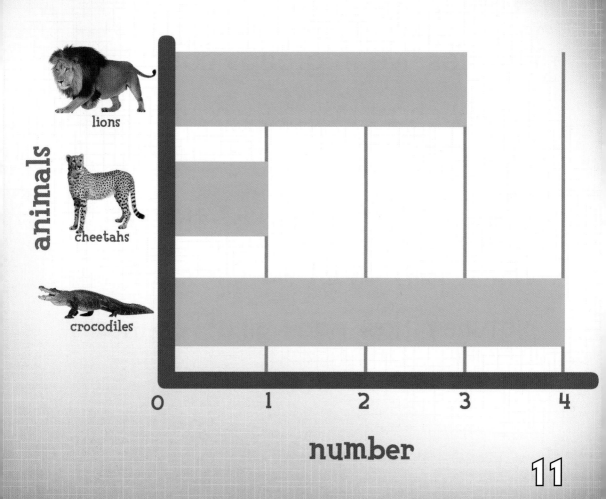

Herds

Giraffes live in groups called herds. A tally chart helps us count a herd.

Look at the picture of the herd. Which tally chart matches the picture? How many giraffes in all?

chart A

how many?	
baby giraffes	/
adult giraffes	//

chart B

how many?	
baby giraffes	//
adult giraffes	////

13

Giraffe herds live on **grasslands** in Africa. Sometimes they walk far to find food.

Look at the two herds. How many tally marks go in the chart for each herd?

herd A

herd B

How Many?	
herd A	
herd B	

Boy giraffes are called bulls.
Girl giraffes are called cows.

Pie graphs show parts of a whole.
Look at the pie graph. How many
bulls are there? How many giraffes
are in the whole herd?

Giraffe Herd

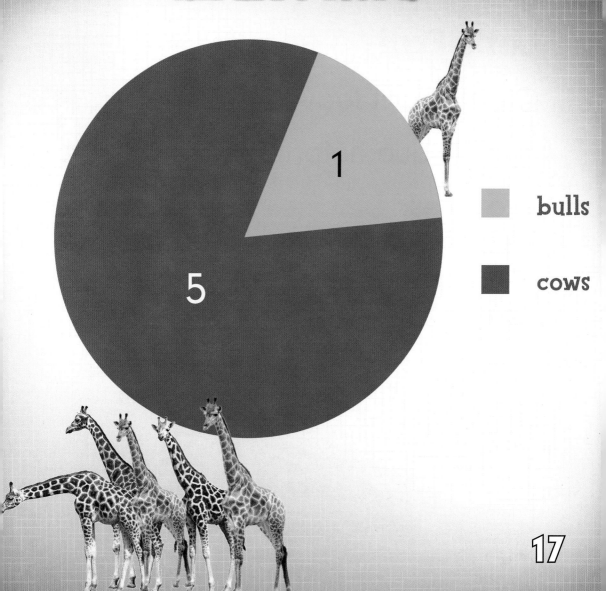

1 — bulls

5 — cows

Let's Eat!

Giraffes eat leaves. Their long neck and tongue help them reach high into trees.

Look at the graph. Which giraffe ate the most? Which giraffe ate 10 leaves?

Hungry Giraffes

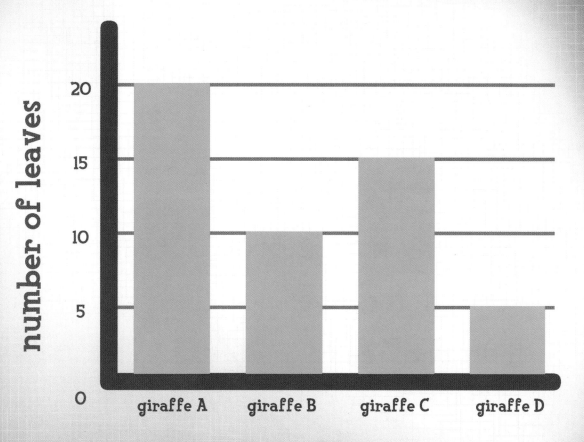

Giraffes have a funny way of drinking water. They need to stand like this giraffe to reach!

Look at the graph. How many more zebras were at the river than giraffes?

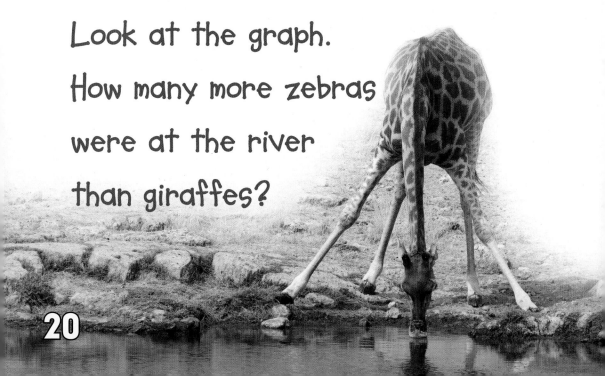

Animals at the River

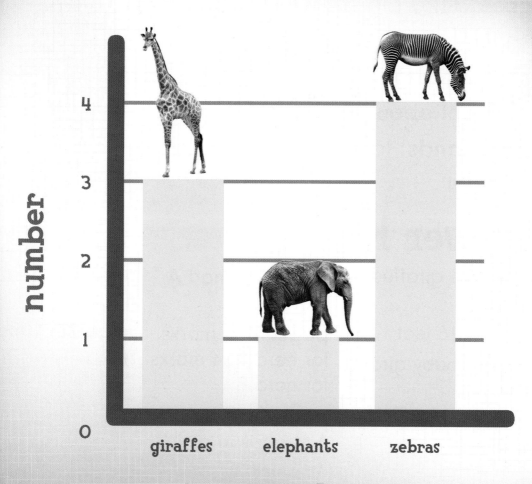

Glossary

cheetah: a big cat with yellow fur and black spots

compare: to find things that are the same and different about two or more things

grasslands: land where grass is the main kind of plant

Answer Key

page 4: 3 giraffes, 4 giraffes

page 6: 16 feet

page 8: baby giraffe, same size

page 10: 3 lions, 1 cheetah

page 12: chart A, 3 giraffes

page 14: 3 marks for herd A, 4 marks for herd B

page 16: 1 bull, 6 giraffes in all

page 18: giraf A, giraffe B

page 20: 1 mo zebra

For More Information

Books

Bodden, Valerie. *Giraffes*. Mankato, MN: Creative Education, 2009.

Pistoia, Sara. *Graphs*. Chanhassen, MN: Child's World, 2007.

Websites

Fractions

www.softschools.com/math/data_analysis/tally_chart/
Practice using a tally chart.

Giraffe

www.zooatlanta.org/home/animals/mammals/giraffe
See photos and watch videos of giraffes.

Index